Cob and Thatch

the inside story

Robert Hesketh

Bossiney Books • Launceston

Fixing the initial layers of thatch with metal crooks

First published 2007 by Bossiney Books Ltd
Langore, Launceston, Cornwall PL15 8LD   www.bossineybooks.com
ISBN 978-189938394-8

Acknowledgements

Several people have helped greatly in the preparation of this book with their advice and expertise, with checking the text and in allowing me to photograph them at work. In particular, I would like to thank Mick Dray (Master Thatcher), David and Glyn Tyler (Jack in the Green), Richard Dray, Alison and Richard Bunning, Jenny Godwin, Steve Pinn, Geoff Codling, Jane Schofield, Jill Smallcombe, Dave Turbitt, Mark Davies, James Davies, Jerome Taylor, Roger Martin, Simon Hallworth, Alan Cameron-Duff, Kevin McCabe and Dave Trant.

Printed in Great Britain by R Booth Ltd, Mabe, Cornwall

Introduction

Cob and thatch buildings are inseparable from the West Country land-scape. With their rounded contours, they look entirely right in their setting, especially if the thatch is of combed wheat reed, finished to the old, unfussy pattern and the cob is left uncovered or given a traditional lime rendering and wash in cream, buff or pink.

Other thatched vernacular buildings using local materials, including granite on Dartmoor and flint with brick in parts of Dorset, blend perfectly into their landscape in the same way. Indeed, cob and thatch come from the very earth and are usually – but not invariably – found together.

This short book explains the essentials of building in, and main-taining, both thatch and cob, putting these fascinating crafts in their historical perspective and intensely local environment.

Thatching and cob walling use inexpensive local materials. They rely on simple hand tools and skills handed on from one generation to the next. Understanding these crafts is not hard, but becoming proficient in them takes time – in the case of thatching, a long apprenticeship and years of practice. The South West remains a stronghold of the thatcher's craft. Devon alone has over 4000 extant thatched buildings, the greatest number in any English county – 17% of the national stock. Dorset, with some 2000 thatched buildings takes second place. Som-erset and even Cornwall have significant numbers too. Most work in thatching today is in rethatching old buildings, either in wheat straw or water reed, but a few new houses are given thatched roofs.

Cob is the West of England term for mass walls of unbaked earth, traditionally built without wickerwork or shuttering, using puddled subsoil, mixed with water and straw. Given 'a good hat and stout boots' – meaning a proper roof and raised stone foundations – and sound maintenance, cob is astonishingly durable. It can last for centuries, as many West Country cob buildings testify.

Cob buildings are found in abundance over large areas of the West that lack good building stone, including great swathes of Devon and the chalk downs of Dorset, as well as parts of Cornwall and Somerset. Indeed, cob is much more widespread than is generally realised be-cause, apart from some garden walls and farm buildings, it is usually hidden under limewash or render.

Cob and thatch buildings at Hope Cove, on the South Devon coast

Earth walling is an ancient skill practised in many parts of Britain without ready access to building stone or brick. There are distinct regional variations, with names such as 'clay lump' in East Anglia, 'mud' in the East Midlands, 'clay dabbin' in Cumbria, 'clom' in Wales and 'wichert' in Buckinghamshire. Worldwide, it has been estimated a third of the world's housing stock has earthen walls. Earth walling and thatch remain the basic building materials for millions of homes, especially in developing nations. However, richer countries have largely abandoned them for less labour intensive but more energy demanding materials and methods that rely heavily on industrial production and cheap transport. Few can match cob and thatch for heat and sound insulation.

Although eclipsed for the past 150 years, cob building remains a living craft in the West Country. This is chiefly through maintaining and repairing existing structures, but there has also been a revival of interest in recent years. Several small cob structures, even houses, have been successfully built using traditional methods.

A historical perspective

It is impossible to say with any accuracy how long cob or thatch has been used. There is no physical evidence of these organic materials in the West Country earlier than the 13th century, though there is evidence of wattle and mud-daub walling from the Iron Age lake villages near Glastonbury and Meare on the Somerset Levels – reconstructions can be seen at the Peat Moors Centre at Westhay near Glastonbury.

Classical authors attest to the use of thatch across Europe. The circular foundations of prehistoric stone houses, which survive in large numbers on Dartmoor and the Cornish moors, are relatively thin and suggest lightweight thatched roofs, though no roofs have survived. By the same reasoning, the Iron Age round house reconstructions at the Peat Moors Centre have conical thatched roofs. We may reasonably infer that both thatch and cob predate the Roman occupation.

Because the methods of building with thatch and cob have remained essentially unchanged in the West Country since at least the 13th century, they provide a strong link with the pre-industrial past and a simpler way of life based on the land and what it could produce.

Thatch and cob buildings are now prized and fetch premium prices, but traditionally these materials had low status. The reaction did not begin until the Arts and Crafts movement in the late 19th century, when a growing appreciation of thatch and cob as part of 'Old England' began to develop among visitors and incomers.

The older view that thatch and cob were inferior and rustic materials is given by several writers, including Cornish historian Richard Carew. Having described the uses of building stone and slate in Cornwall, Carew wrote in 1602: 'The poor cottager contenteth himself with cob for his walls, and thatch for his covering.' Carew's remarks could equally have been applied to other western counties. He was clearly aware of a social distinction in building materials.

Thatch and cob were certainly cheap and widely used, especially for humble dwellings, garden walls and farm buildings. Unfortunately, the farm buildings in particular have not always been properly maintained and large numbers have gone.

Many more cob buildings have lost the thatched roofs they originally had, as old photographs reveal. Corrugated iron has long been a cheaper alternative to thatch, which is fortunate in one respect: more

North Bovey, on Dartmoor, where granite and thatch were the norm

farm buildings built of cob might otherwise have gone roofless and been lost.

However, more prestigious buildings such as parsonages, inns and substantial farmhouses with cob walls were also commonly thatched, and a disproportionate number of them survive, chiefly because they were well built in the first place. Even manor houses were sometimes constructed in cob and thatch. Sir Walter Raleigh's birthplace, Hayes Barton near East Budleigh, Devon is a fine example.

On Dartmoor, granite and thatch was more usual for both farm buildings and farm houses, especially among the longhouses characteristic of that area, in which the shippon (animal quarters) was under the same roof as the farmhouse and only separated from it by a cross passage. There is thought to be only one true thatched cob longhouse – Flood Farm at Drewsteignton on the eastern edge of Dartmoor.

In areas with good local quarries stone rather than cob was often the natural choice for walling. As Carew noted, this included large areas of Cornwall, with its sandstone and granite. It also included such bastions of stone building as Dartmoor, where much of the granite could be collected from the surface, and the Mendips with their limestone quarries. South Somerset is dominated by golden Ham stone and South Dorset by its Portland stone. Bath is a city of such characteristic material that it is simply called 'Bath Stone'.

Similarly, settlements near slate quarries traditionally have slate roofs. This encompasses much of Cornwall and West Devon. Places like Bridgwater, near brick kilns or tile works, used those materials, whilst sea ports such as Plymouth, Topsham and Exeter could ship in slate and tile, as well as brick and stone, far more cheaply than anywhere inland.

It was not until the national railway network spread, between 1840 and 1900, that bulk goods could be transported cheaply to almost every corner of the country. The net result was a large scale loss of local building traditions and a dramatic decline in the use of some materials including thatch, cob and locally quarried stone.

For this reason, most cob and thatch buildings in the West (and elsewhere in Britain) date from between 1400 and 1850. This was the great period of vernacular building, when most structures were built by local craftsmen using local materials and designs. These materials and designs were dictated by practical considerations such as cost and availability, but the result is very pleasing to the eye and the buildings are integral to each region's character.

Cob walls are often found matched with slate or tile roofs, sometimes in the countryside but particularly in towns which have suffered severe fires. In most cases thatch was the original roofing material and the heavier slate or tile roofs were added later. Often this necessitated stronger roofing timbers and sometimes strengthening of the cob walls with buttressing.

There were various reasons for replacing thatch with slate or tile. Although prestigious and much sought after today, thatch was long considered old fashioned and rustic. As slate and tile became more widely available with the railways, thatch seemed obsolete.

It had lost its main practical advantage, relative cheapness, whilst retaining its chief disadvantage, vulnerability to fire – which was long reflected in high, often prohibitively high, insurance premiums. These offered another strong incentive to abandon thatch.

It was only during the 20th century that modern fire fighting services, building regulations and a decline in the number of open hearths gradually reduced the vulnerability of thatched buildings to fire and insurance companies began to offer more reasonable policies.

Tiverton is a good example of a Devon town that once had a high proportion of thatched buildings, but suffered a series of disastrous fires. The town lost some four hundred houses to fire in 1598, six hundred in 1612 and a further 298 in 1731. Fires were also recorded in 1661 and 1730. After the 1731 conflagration, thatch was banned in Tiverton. An Act was passed ordering that all roofs should be of slate, lead or tile. There were no more major fires.

Crediton, also in mid-Devon, suffered a disastrous fire in 1743, in which eighteen people died and 460 dwellings were destroyed. It bears strong similarities to the Great Fire of London, beginning in a baker's shop and spreading rapidly through narrow streets of terraced houses, fanned by a powerful wind.

Traditional methods of containing fire, such as ripping away thatched roofs with special hooked poles, proved ineffective. As in London in 1666, a fire break was created by blowing up houses – but even this did not stop the Crediton flames.

An important map survives showing Crediton as it was before the 1743 fire. It depicts a mix of houses of various dates. Some of the larger 18th century buildings were brick and slate – the new national style of architecture we now call Georgian demanded these materials. However, the older and humbler houses were mainly thatched and, by inference, of cob.

Although small West Country towns with a high proportion of thatch and cob buildings can be found, such as Moretonhampstead and Hatherleigh in Devon, they were much more numerous in the past. Several Devon towns which are noted today for the number of their historic buildings, including Totnes, Ashburton and Dartmouth, are also remarkable for their slate roofs, and it was these which tended to preserve the town from destructive fires.

Groups of thatch and cob buildings have more often survived in villages, partly because smaller groups of houses are less vulnerable to fire, partly because of rural conservatism. There are many splendid examples in Devon, spread liberally around the county, but most densely in mid- and East Devon, the Exe Valley and the eastern flank of Dartmoor.

Silverton in the Exe Valley has several buildings and a late medieval street of cob and thatch – despite serious fires in 1837 and 1878.

The Drum Inn at Cockington was designed by Sir Edward Lutyens

Hope Cove in the South Hams has a handsome square of cob and thatch, whilst the East Devon estate villages of Broadhembury and Broadclyst provide a wonderful uniformity of cream coloured houses in these materials. Otterton and Branscombe, close to the Dorset border, have exceptionally long streets of cob and thatch, whilst Morchard Bishop in mid-Devon is said to have England's longest terrace of thatched cottages.

The minor revival in thatch brought about by the Arts and Crafts movement in the late 19th and early 20th centuries also left its mark in Devon. The best examples can be seen in the architect-designed *cottages ornés* of Budleigh Salterton and the thatched Drum Inn. This was designed by Sir Edwin Lutyens and built at that much improved and much visited thatched village, Cockington near Torquay. Neither the Drum nor the Budleigh Salterton villas are Devon vernacular, but they have their own beauty and historic interest.

In Dorset some of the best examples of cob and thatch, such as the hamlet of Plush and Thomas Hardy's birthplace (National Trust) at Higher Bockhampton, are found among the chalky uplands, where cob is often called 'mud'. Milton Abbas is exceptional. Created in 1780 by Lord Dorchester after he demolished the original village (because it obstructed his lordly views) it is entirely cob and thatch.

Cob and thatch can be found in several parts of Somerset, especially on the red Keuper marls and towards the Devon border on Exmoor, where East Quantoxhead, Bossington and Selworthy (National Trust) offer some of the county's best examples. The old town of Minehead is a hidden gem of thatch. However, on the Levels and in river valleys many cob buildings have been lost to floods.

Cornwall – pre-eminently a county of stone, especially granite – has a spread of farm buildings and some houses in both thatch and cob, mainly along the Devon border and on the Lizard. Cob is also found under slate roofs and slate wall cladding, characteristic of Cornwall and West Devon.

Thatch

Unlike cob, thatch cannot be mistaken for any other material, though not all thatch is the same. With three distinctive types of thatch – combed wheat reed, long straw and water reed – and a variety of local traditions and styles, there is a great deal more to thatching than first meets the eye. To the practised observer, these distinctions and even the work of individual thatchers stand apart.

Most thatched roofs, like most cob walls, originated well before 1900 and the imposition of a few uniform building styles across the country. Thatching, once merely utilitarian, is now valued for its associations with tradition, pre-industrial farming methods and a near vanished rural way of life.

For all that, thatching is very much a living craft, particularly in the West Country. More thatch has survived here than elsewhere, though thatched buildings were once common in large areas of the country south of a line from the Mersey to the Wash.

Undoubtedly thatching is an ancient craft, though (like cob building) it is impossible to date its origin and the oldest examples have almost certainly perished. However, there is firm evidence for medieval thatch. Although thatch must be periodically repaired and renewed because it decays, it is traditional to 'overcoat' West Country roofs if the thatch is not rotted right through. This means stripping off the decayed upper thatch, whilst leaving the base coat on. In time, a number of base coats may build up. However, it is usual practice to make the

Roof timbers and thatch blackened with soot deposits from open fires, at the Church House, South Tawton

pitch of the roof steeper by completely stripping the lower layers near the eaves.

How long a thatched roof will last before it needs to be repaired, overcoated or replaced depends upon many things, including the location of the building, the local climate and the pitch of the roof. Whilst the upper levels of thatch may be renewed at an average of fifteen to thirty years in the wet and windy West Country (fifty or sixty years is sometimes claimed for roofs in drier East Anglia), base coats may be old, even as old as the buildings themselves because of overcoating.

Thus a building may have medieval thatch. If it began as an 'open hall house' without a chimney, in which wood smoke was left to percolate out through the roof, the thatch and the roof timbers may be blackened with ancient soot deposits. The roof timbers to which the thatch is fixed can be dated accurately by dendrochronology (tree ring dating) and carbon dating techniques for thatch are being developed.

Ancient thatch also provides a fascinating record of the crops grown and used for thatching in the past, especially when the ears were left on the stalks. Sometimes, weeds survive among the straw. Written historical records on this subject are almost non-existent, so thatch is a rich source of special archaeological evidence.

A 'half-nitch' consisting of four bundles of combed wheat reed

Thatching with water reed at Kenn

Time has many hazards and thatch is prone to rot as well as fire. Medieval smoke blackened roofs are rare (Devon has around 180), but can be seen in a few buildings open to the public. Notable among these are the Church House, South Tawton and Marker's Cottage, Broadclyst, both in Devon (see pages 26-27).

'Combed wheat reed' (also known as 'combed straw'), as distinct from 'long straw' and water reed, is the traditional West Country thatching material. Today, it is nearly always wheat straw, specially grown from old fashioned varieties with long, strong, straight stems. However, analysis of smoke blackened medieval thatch shows that many other fibres were formerly used. Rye was common and sometimes heather, pea rods, ferns, broom and furze (gorse) were made to serve. Probably thatchers used whatever was locally available.

Combed wheat reed is a distinctively West Country thatching tradition, though why that should be so is a subject of debate. Perhaps straw was prized and treated carefully because cereal crops were marginal over much of the West, where a wet climate favours animal husbandry. Farmers combed short straws and rubbish from each 'nitch' or straw bundle before thatching with it or even using it for bedding. Before the 19th century, combing was by hand. Mechanisation began with hand cranked reed combers. Later models were horse- or tractor-driven and attached to threshing machines.

Wheat or rye for combed reed is harvested by hand or with a reaper/ binder so as not to bruise it, with the thicker butt ends of the stems all facing one way. The thatcher lays the straw with the butt ends of combed wheat reed facing outwards so that the thatch has a uniform appearance.

The second thatching tradition uses 'crushed straw' also known as 'long straw'. Practised in the Midlands and the South East, this gives a distinctly different roof, identifiable by its shaggier appearance, with lengths of straw visible and ears of corn protruding. This is because the straw, although from the same wheat and rye varieties as combed wheat reed, has been treated differently. It is often bruised during harvesting and the butt ends are mixed up with the ear ends.

Thatching in water reed forms a third tradition. Once largely confined to East Anglia where reed grows abundantly in the extensive marshes, it was rare in the western counties before the Second World War. Water reed is now increasingly popular because of its reputation for durability.

Whilst the relative merits of water reed and combed wheat reed are much debated, it is often hard to tell them apart from ground level, especially if (as is often the case in the West Country) the water reed has been overcoated in the same fashion as combed wheat reed. The techniques of thatching in combed wheat reed and water reed are generally similar, as I found talking to Devon thatcher Mick Dray from Lustleigh on the eastern fringe of Dartmoor.

'I've had a fantastic life in thatching,' said Mick, whose family has been in the trade for five generations. 'It's a slow process. You really need five years to learn thatching because you only completely rethatch ten or a dozen roofs in one year.' Mick served the usual five-year thatcher's apprenticeship with his father when he left school in 1963.

Left: Nigel Lister of Chagford with unsplit hazel rods
Right: Mark Davies, twisting a spar into shape

Many of Mick's tools and materials are local. His spar hooks and shearing hooks used to be made at the Finch Foundry in Sticklepath and now come from Morris of Dunsford, whilst his hazel spars are cut at Moretonhampstead.

'Spars are like a massive wooden staple. You buy them in one length, twist them and they strengthen the roof,' Mick explained. 'The metal crooks we use to hold down the initial layers used to be made by local blacksmiths. Some were $3/8$" thick, but the rods we use now are thinner, say $1/4$".'

Mick Dray sticks to his time honoured stock of thatcher's tools. Most are traditional, but 'leggetts', the paddle shaped tools used to flatten straw onto the roof, making it more watertight as well as neater, have changed somewhat. They used to be made of wood, but water reed is so tough that it soon wears them out. Mick now uses cast aluminium leggetts, but these are still made to the traditional pattern, with grooves cut across to grip the reed.

Mick Dray (in the foreground) dressing thatch with a leggett, whilst Richard Dray behind him is fastening spars with a mallet

James Davies trimming thatch with shears

For lightness and durability, Mick also uses aluminium ladders instead of the old wooden ones. Combined with scaffolding (Drays do their own), these have made thatching safer and less onerous.

A thatcher's pole ladder, bevelled to enable a man to stand on it for long periods, is another must. Reeding needles to pin the thatch back, sheep shears to trim wheat straw, garden shears, a mallet for driving home the spars and a butcher's knife for tough cutting complete the kit.

Modern varieties of wheat are too short and weak and too battered by combine harvesters to be of any use for combed wheat reed. Local thatchers use wheat specially grown for thatching in Devon from traditional varieties, such as Maris Widgeon, Maris Huntsman, N59,

Most thatchers' tools
are traditional, but a
modern cordless drill is
very useful.
This is Dave Turbitt,
thatching at Whimple

Using a billhook to
split a hazel rod for
spars

Combed wheat reed is
prepared from wheat
traditionally reaped
and stooked, as here at
Sidbury in East Devon

Square Head Master, Red Standard and White Victor. These are chosen for their long, strong stems and small ears.

The wheat is still cut with an old-fashioned reaper/binder and stooked up in the fields. It is left for two weeks in stook to dry slowly and evenly, and then put into the rick before going on to the threshing machine. Here, the short straws are combed out and the grain and chaff removed. The long stems are kept perfectly straight. Finally, the straw is trussed up and bundled.

'It's a labour intensive job,' said Mick, who keeps his own collection of traditional machinery in working order and loans it to farmers in return for cut price straw. 'Unfortunately, there's less and less labour you can call on. It's no good having someone who's inexperienced.'

Traditionally, English thatchers obtained water reed from Norfolk. However, nitrate run-off has polluted many of the watercourses and reed beds, causing the reed to outgrow its strength. Norfolk thatchers buy up most of the remaining pockets of good reed for themselves.

This means that most water reed has to be imported to meet the demand from the rest of Britain, which cannot be met by home grown wheat reed alone. Mick has travelled widely to Holland, Poland and Hungary to buy high quality reed. Austria used to be a good source, but there have been pollution problems there too. Recent buying trips have taken him far into central Turkey, where nitrates are unknown, but bandits are not and an armed guard was provided.

We turned to the contentious topic of combed wheat reed as opposed to water reed. Which Mick recommends depends upon the property he is working on: 'There are some buildings water reed just doesn't lend itself to – it doesn't look right. I like working in both materials.

'Thatch will hold up against slate any day. A thatched roof is not only well insulated, but sound proofed as well. These days, insurance is very competitive and thatch can be insured for only a fraction more.'

He is confident that thatching has a good future: 'Things will change, but thatching itself probably won't. Being on the Executive Council of the National Society of Master Thatchers, I look on thatching more as a national issue than a local issue, though I'm also a member of the Devon and Cornwall Master Thatchers. One of the reasons I like travelling is I meet some great people. I think having a wider perspective is a lot better than just bumbling along.'

Cob

The large number of West Country cob buildings and their geographical spread surprises most people. Because cob is usually covered in render, it is often hard to distinguish from stone or brick – even professional surveyors and builders have been known to mistake one material for another.

Where cob is left exposed, usually in farm buildings or garden walls, it is easily identified, though its colour varies greatly with the soil used. If covered, cob is most readily told apart by four things. First of all there is the exceptional wall thickness – between two and four feet at the base, but usually tapering to half that at the eaves. Such thickness is necessary for the stability of mass earth walling.

Secondly, cob buildings were usually built low to reduce the weight and mass of the walls. Three storey cob houses are unusual, two storeys are more common. For the same reasons, the ceilings are traditionally low, often lower than modern building regulations would allow for a new house. Thirdly, cob walls have rounded corners because sharp edges are both difficult to achieve and more prone to erosion.

Then there is the plinth, traditionally of stone, though brick and latterly concrete blocks have been used successfully. Plinths are found beneath almost all cob walls, which normally protrude a few inches beyond them so that rainwater can drip directly to the ground. To protect cob against rising damp and splash-back at ground level from gutterless roofs, plinths are raised a foot or more above ground level, though in North Devon and Cornwall they may reach to the first floor. Except on farm buildings, plinths are often rendered and, traditionally, covered in black pitch.

Cob is unbaked earth. It is hard and durable so long as it is kept dry – though the excessive dryness given by a damp course (sometimes unwisely insisted upon by insurance companies) may cause it to shrink and crack. Water penetration will eventually turn cob back to mud and it will disintegrate. Thus it needs 'stout boots' in the form of a plinth to protect it from groundwater.

Equally, it requires a 'good hat'. Traditionally this is a thatched roof, which is light and easily supported by cob walls. Given a generous overhang, thatch will throw rainwater clear of the walls without guttering. As we saw in the last section, thatch is an excellent material, but

This old farm building has in the past been rendered with concrete – quicker and cheaper but ultimately less effective than traditonal lime rendering because it cracks. The roof, by contrast, has at least done its job well, regardless of appearances

requires regular maintenance and more frequent replacement than other roof coverings.

Subsoil, water and straw are the raw ingredients of cob. To save time and labour, the soil was dug and the cob mixed on site wherever possible. This is in stark contrast to modern building practice with industrially produced materials, which involves high energy expenditure in manufacturing and transport, thus leaving a large 'environmental footprint'. Cob's most obvious footprints are the pits that sometimes survive as depressions in the ground. Often, these pits were used as ready-dug privies or, filled with water, as duckponds.

Soils vary in their chemical composition, clay and stone content. Some make stronger cob than others. The ideal soil has 15-25% clay to give it plasticity and a strong lime (calcium carbonate) element. A good mix of aggregate and sand will also improve its strength and durability. The calcium carbonate is of particular importance in hardening the mix, which is why the chalky soils found in parts of Dorset and East Devon make particularly good cob.

Several different cobs can be identified, especially in Devon with its complex geology, ranging from pink or red on the red sandstones, through ochre and buff on the culm measures, to grey on the chalk.

Chopped straw acts as a binding agent, preventing cracking as the cob slowly dries out and also adding extra calcium carbonate. Achieving the correct consistency means adding the right amount of straw and water for the type of soil used. Sometimes, extra aggregates or sand may be added to the raw cob to reduce shrinkage and increase weather resistance and compressive strength.

Mixing cob the old (and hard) way on a Devon Rural Skills Trust course

The cob must then be mixed thoroughly, traditionally by treading. Without the assistance of cattle or other heavy animals, treading glutinous cob was very hard labour. A tractor does the job as well and much quicker!

In mixing cob and checking its consistency, there is no substitute for experience. Equally, judging the required thickness of a cob wall, how much it may safely taper towards the eaves and how much cob can be applied on each 'raise' or 'lift' are skills acquired by long practice. A 'raise' is usually a foot or two at the most. It is the height which can be added to the cob wall at one time without compromising its capacity to stay firm and dry out naturally. After a raise, the wall must be covered and left to dry thoroughly before the next raise is added. Distinct horizontal banding left by this process can be seen in some cob walls.

The time gap between each raise is very variable depending on weather conditions, but might be measured in weeks or even months. Winter is generally too cold and wet to allow proper drying. Thus it is best to begin building a cob wall in spring and finish it by late autumn. Although the process might be stretched over two years if the summer is wet, Devon builder Kevin McCabe, who has built several new cob houses, has found one season sufficient for raising the walls. However, an extra week is needed before adding the roof and Kevin recommends waiting another six months before fitting windows and door frames to allow for extra shrinkage in the cob. Thus, he allows fifteen months from start to finish for a new cob house.

Historically, it made sense for the cob walling team – usually four men – to build several walls in rotation, letting one dry out whilst adding a raise to another. As the team were usually rural labourers seasonally engaged in various work, they would in any case stop for important tasks like planting, mowing and harvesting. All these tasks – and cob walling too – usually had a communal flavour.

Such a small scale, leisurely and irregular working pattern is completely at odds with modern house building in industrialised countries (though it continues unaltered in much of the Third World). Today, speed is of the essence and contracts are governed by deadlines. Large housing estates yield the greatest economy of scale in a market dominated by huge national or international building companies.

However, there has been a revival of West Country cob building over the last twenty years, albeit on a modest scale, as I discovered at a Devon Rural Skills Trust (DRST) cob walling event. Experienced cob wall builders were sharing their skills with a number of learners, some of whom were completely new to the craft.

It was a fine, dry spring day at Hatherland Mill Farm in the Exe Valley near Bampton, just right for the task in hand – building a garden wall of cob. A plinth of concrete blocks had already been built and the first raise laid some weeks before. Penned in with a suitable mix of subsoil from a nearby pit mixed with surplus straw, the farm's herd of Dexter cattle had already trodden a considerable quantity of cob over the previous five days.

More soil and straw was mixed with a judicious helping of water by DRST tutors Jenny Godwin and Steve Pinn. The group were then invited to put the boot in and tread the cob. Jenny tried the mix several times with a garden fork before she was satisfied it had reached the right consistency.

The group divided. Those working at ground level raised forkfuls of cob to people on top of the wall. Some stamped it into place, others used heavy wooden mallets and even cricket bats to shape the wall and smooth the edges. Surplus cob was pared off with spades and knives, and then reused.

It was very enjoyable work – and physically tiring. Tutor David Tyler came to the rescue, mixing another load of cob by driving his tractor back and forth over it, before heaving it up on the wall with the foreloader. It was a small concession to modern technology.

Another group were meanwhile repairing a heavily weathered cob barn. Their first task was making unbaked clay blocks by hand, using wooden forms – a method similar to making 'clay lump' in East Anglia

Lifting raw cob onto the top of the wall

Consolidating the mud is vital, and is done both by stamping on the top of the 'raise' and beating it from both sides

and adobe in many regions of the world. Whilst these blocks hardened off in the sun, the group made cob mortar to a more plastic consistency than the cob for the wall. This mortar alone was sufficient to fill in some of the smaller gaps in the wall, whilst the clay blocks, secured with the mortar, filled the bigger gaps.

Cob is a versatile material, as Hatherland Mill Farm's owners, architect and conservation specialist Alison Bunning and her husband, Richard, explained. The Bunnings are convinced of cob's practical worth, its heat and sound insulating properties and its durability.

Hatherland Mill Farm began as a thatched 'open hall' house around 1400, the ceiling, chimney and second storey being later refinements. Parts of the walls are stone, part cob – but not all the cob is medieval.

At Hatherland Mill Farm, the house extension has been built in cob, but to a modern design. The sculpted cob staircase is a special feature, as is the massive cob chimney breast, which includes built-in alcoves. The chimney breast is finished in Devon red earth plaster and polished with beeswax. Its attractive crazing was a happy accident, the result of the drying process during which natural salts leached through hairline cracks in the plaster

As well as the garden wall, the earth plaster oven in the garden is modern, though to a very old design. It has proved its worth baking bread and cooking pizzas and barbeques.

The house extension is also to traditional design, but combines old fashioned cob construction with modern technology, including heat exchangers and thermostats, as its builders, David and Glyn Tyler explained. Having studied historic buildings in depth and practised as an archaeologist, David Tyler wanted to build in traditional materials himself. Thus, he and his brother Glyn make their living with their firm Jack in the Green.

'I don't see the building we do these days as all that dissimilar from buildings archaeology,' said David. 'This is heritage work. We try to conserve what is conservable and feel very privileged to be involved.'

All the jobs undertaken by Jack in the Green have been restoring traditional West Country buildings. This is what the Tylers particularly like, though they have a high regard for builders such as Kevin McCabe and Jeremy and Jan Sharpe who have created entirely new thatch and cob houses.

'A lot of it comes from having a love of what you're doing,' said Glyn, a carpenter who became disenchanted with the noise, pressure and machismo of big building sites. 'Features that we have noticed and liked in local buildings, we recreate in our own building. Cob buildings feel comfortable and welcoming. I've yet to walk into a cob house and feel I didn't want to be there.

'We can walk away from every job we do thinking, *I like that*. We're firmly in the vernacular building tradition, sticking with traditional building materials because we enjoy working with them – know and like the look of them.'

'It's so much nicer working with traditional materials,' added David. 'Cob is so much more flexible than cement. You can make curves with it, sculpt it like clay. The only limits are money and your imagination.

'We take a holistic approach to building and are very interested in ecological issues,' he continued. 'We are also involved in working with green oak, hedge laying and coppicing, mainly with Devon Rural Skills Trust. We like to be involved with every element of the Devon landscape. Hopefully, our building work complements that landscape and is not alien to it like so much modern building.'

The Tylers also work with lime render, wash and plaster, materials that naturally accompany their work with cob. Except when left exposed in low value constructions such as garden walls and farm buildings, cob was traditionally covered either with protective lime render, or else just with limewash routinely applied. Indeed, lime, mortar, plaster and render were used in all types of building before cement (derived from fired chalk and clay) became widely available during the 19th century. Cement quickly gained popularity in the increasingly industrialized building trade because of the speed with which it could be mixed and applied.

As Glyn and David explained, the great advantage of lime products over cement is that they allow cob to 'breathe'. This prevents the wall either drying out excessively and cracking, or losing its strength through becoming waterlogged with trapped moisture. Equally, lime is less likely to crack because it is less brittle than sand and cement and the wall it covers is less prone to excessive shrinkage and swelling. Lime has the additional advantage of maintaining a level of humidity inside the building that is pleasanter and healthier for people too.

Lime derived from burnt limestone can be used as render, wash, mortar, pointing and plaster. The essential difference between these forms is the relative proportions of lime to sand, earth and water.

Lime render, commonly made with three parts sand to one part lime, can be cast on to cob walls, prepared by removing dust and debris with a stiff brush and wetting the surface. It is covered with up to six coats of limewash, made of one part lime to two parts water. Again, the limewash is applied to a wetted surface and each coat must be allowed to dry before the next is applied, a time consuming process, which pays dividends in protecting the wall.

An interior wall covering of lime plaster is also historically correct for cob, aesthetically pleasing and practical. Lime preparations come in a variety of colours, pink, cream and buff being traditional in the West Country. The principles and practice of using lime in building are explained with clarity and simplicity by Jane Schofield in *Lime in Building*, companion to her *Cob Buildings* (see bibliography). As with cob walling, the equipment needed is surprisingly simple, including buckets, brushes and trowels that many householders already posses. However, a mixer fitted to an electric drill or a cement mixer saves a lot of hard labour.

'If you know how to plaster with modern materials, you'll find lime plastering vernacular buildings broadly similar,' said Glyn. 'You can mix your own lime and sometimes we do, but it's easier to buy it ready mixed and you can be sure of the consistency. Half an inch is the ideal thickness for lime plaster, but there is a large measure of leeway from this optimum. But like cob, lime needs the right climatic conditions to set. Winter's not ideal.'

How, I asked, should people learn the necessary skills to work with cob and lime?

'Books are useful,' said David, 'but it's very difficult to completely convey skills on paper. There's nothing to beat experience. We're great fans of courses. We enjoy the camaraderie, talking to people and exchanging ideas. Cob walling is all about getting involved. We aim to keep traditional skills alive and pass them on to other people.'

David and Glyn are confident of having plenty of work to keep them in business. They are confident too that traditional, sustainable building materials have a good future.

'I think that there's vast scope for sustainable building,' said David, 'especially as people become more environmentally aware, and the rising cost of fuel pushes up the price of industrially produced building materials. This will hopefully make recycled, sustainable and locally produced materials more viable. Cob and thatch will have a contribution to make in this movement.'

Conclusion

Thatch and cob have a long history in the West Country. They also have a future. At the least, this will involve maintaining our rich inheritance of historic buildings. Roofing in thatch and walling in cob will remain living traditions so long as traditional skills are passed on to the next generation. In the first place this depends upon the owners of thatched cob and stone buildings keeping their properties in good repair, particularly by regular rethatching, which creates the necessary demand for skilled labour.

Much of the region's past can be read directly from its thatched buildings of cob and stone. It is therefore vital not only to maintain these buildings, but preserve their integrity, especially when adding extensions and modernisations. These need to be in suitable materials and of the right scale and style to harmonise with traditional buildings.

Rural skills organisations and some traditional builders do an excellent job in teaching vernacular building crafts, including cob wall building. In doing so, they raise interest and pride in these skills, encouraging home owners to preserve their vernacular buildings for the future.

The future will also include new thatched and earthen buildings – and not only in Britain. The recent West Country resurgence in thatch and cob has been mirrored elsewhere, notably in the western United States, Canada and New Zealand, where the sculptural potential of cob has been exploited to create some highly imaginative yet practical homes with unconventional curves and built-in cob furniture.

Thatch and cob have been used to build a small number of new West Country houses over the past twenty years, as well as occasional garden walls and cloam ovens. Marker's Cottage (National Trust) at

Broadclyst, Devon has a beautifully sculpted cob summerhouse with a conical thatched roof. Like Down St Mary in Devon and Stithians in Cornwall, Broadclyst also boasts a thatched cob bus shelter.

With ever rising fuel and transport costs and general acknowledgement of the immense ecological damage done by carbon emissions, thatched roofs and earthen walls show to great advantage against industrially produced building materials, which exact a high environmental price in both manufacture and transport. Thatch and cob also offer excellent insulation, reducing year on year energy demands.

However, whilst the relative cost of industrial building materials may increase, it seems highly unlikely thatch and cob will be able to provide any major alternative in the drive to provide millions of new homes, offices and factories in the developed world. Speed and supply are the main problems, but building regulations also have to be carefully negotiated when building a new house with a thatched roof or cob walls.

The slow, weather-dependent nature of building in thatch and cob may be acceptable on small scale projects where the customer can afford to wait and the builder can divert to other work for a wet spell, or even the entire winter, but this will not answer on big building projects with their schedules and deadlines. Even with mechanisation of laborious work such as mixing and lifting cob or combing wheat reed, traditional building methods remain irremediably slow compared with precast concrete and sheet glass.

Supplies of local wheat reed, specially grown from traditional varieties, cut by a reaper/binder, stooked by hand, then threshed and combed with a slow, old fashioned machine, are already inadequate to meet the needs of West Country thatchers, who go further and further abroad to buy good water reed. A major increase in demand for thatch could not be met without new sources of supply either of wheat or water reed. A steady supply of thatch is essential to meet the need to repair and replace existing roofs. Such repair and replacement is far from cheap and a major deterrent to using thatch on new buildings.

Although the supply of subsoil for cob is not a problem in those extensive West Country areas with suitable geology, cob has a number of inherent disadvantages, limiting its likely use in the future. The greatest disadvantages are that it is slow to work with and labour intensive. It also needs weather protection. The quickest solution, concrete

Left: The Friends' Meeting House, at Come-to-Good between Carnon Downs and the King Harry Ferry

render, is unsuitable because it is liable to cracking and provokes both shrinkage and water logging.

Thatch and cob are highly unlikely to be used again on a large scale, except in the Third World, but their environmental cost is minimal; they blend wonderfully into the West Country landscape and offer excellent heat and sound insulation. These are strong recommendations for retaining and reviving the use of thatch and cob, which will both have their parts to play in the sustainable buildings of the future.

Thatch, cob and stone buildings open to the public

Many West Country towns and villages are noted for their thatched cob or stone buildings; some are inns, often listed for their historical value. There is only space here for a selection, plus a range of other thatched buildings open privately or through the National Trust and English Heritage. Where buildings are not open to the public, please respect the owners' privacy.

A remarkably deep overhanging roof at Sampford Courtenay, near Okehampton, Devon

The Forge at Branscombe in East Devon, maintained by the National Trust

Cornwall

Towns and villages: Helford, Lizard Town (especially Church Cove), St Clement, Veryan with its round houses.

Inns: Crantock, Old Albion; Helford, Shipwright's Arms; Helston, Blue Anchor; Mylor Bridge, Pandora Inn

Devon

Towns and villages: Atherington, Bickleigh, Branscombe, Broadclyst, Broadhembury, Budleigh Salterton, Chagford, Chittlehampton, Cockington, Colyton, Croyde, Drewsteignton, Dunsford, East Budleigh, Gittisham, Hatherleigh, Hope Cove, Lustleigh, Morchard Bishop, Moretonhampstead, Newton Poppleford, North Bovey, Otterton, Sampford Courtenay, Sidbury, Silverton, South Tawton, South Zeal, Sticklepath, Stokeinteignhead, Thorverton, Whimple, Winkleigh

Inns: Chagford, Three Crowns; Christow, Artichoke; Cockington, Drum Inn; Dartington, Cott Inn; Dalwood, Tucker's Arms; Highampton, Golden Inn; Horn's Cross, Hoops Inn; Knowstone, Mason's Arms; Silverton, Three Tuns; Start Bay, Start Bay Inn; Yealmpton, Old Mother Hubbard's Restaurant
National Trust: Branscombe Forge and Bakery 01297 68033 and 680481; Loughwood Meeting House 01392 881691; Broadclyst, Marker's Cottage 01392 461546

Dorset

Towns and villages: Abbotsbury, Bere Regis, Farnham, Milton Abbas, Okeford Fitzpaine, Piddletrenthide, Plush, Tolpuddle
Inns: Corfe Mullen, Coventry Arms; East Lulworth, Weld Arms; Godmanstone, Smith's Arms; Shave Cross, Shave Cross Inn; Stoborough, King's Arms (with sections of earth walling displayed through a screen); Sturminster Newton, White Hart
National Trust: Hardy's Cottage, Higher Bockhampton (NT) 01305 262366

Somerset

Towns and villages: Bossington, East Quantoxhead, Minehead (old town), Porlock, Selworthy
Inns: Castle Cary, George; Curry Rivel, Olde Forge Inn; Porlock Weir, Ship Inn; Westonzoyland, Sedgemoor Inn (tiled roof, but sections of wattle and daub displayed through a screen); Winsford, Royal Oak

Opposite: The Fox Inn, Corscombe, Dorset   Above: Selworthy in Somerset

English Heritage: Muchelney Abbey (thatched latrine) 01458 250664
National Trust: High Ham, Stembridge Tower Mill (thatched windmill);
Muchelney, Priest's House. 01458 253771; Selworthy, shop and tea rooms
Peat Moors Centre, Westhay 01458 860697 (reconstructions of Iron Age
houses with wattle, daub and thatch)

For more information

The details were correct at the time of printing but are subject to change.

Centre for Earthen Architecture, University of Plymouth School of
    Architecture, The Hoe Centre, Notte Street, Plymouth PL1 2AR
    01752 233634 www.tech.plym.ac.uk/soa/arch/earth.htm
Cob in Cornwall, Manaccan, Helston, Cornwall TR12 6EN 01326 231773
    www.cobincornwall.com
Cornwall Sustainable Building Trust, Eden's Watering Lane Nursery, Lobb's
    Shop, St Austell, Cornwall PL26 6BE 01726 686 www.csbt.org.uk
Devon Earth Building Association, South Combe, Cheriton Fitzpaine,
    Crediton, Devon EX17 4HP www.devonearthbuilding.com
Devon Rural Skills Trust: Mick Godfrey, Chiltern, Horner, Halwell, Totnes,
    Devon TQ9 7LB 01548 821156
Devon and Cornwall Master Thatchers Association: Alan Prince, Foxhole,
    Hillside, South Brent, Devon TQ10 9 AU

Dorset Master Thatchers Association: Nigel Turton, Park Cottage, Tollard Royal, Salisbury, Wilts

Dorset Centre for Rural Skills, West Farm Barn, Farrington, Blandford, Dorset DT11 8RA   01747 811099   www.dorsetruralskills.co.uk

GR Dray, Master Thatchers, Bishopstone, Caseley Lane, Lustleigh, Devon TQ13 9TN   01647 277293

Earthed World (Cob Walling): Earthed, Flat 1, Drewsteignton, Devon EX6 6QP   0791 7361579   earthed@macunlimited.net

Kevin McCabe (builds new and repairs old cob houses): Keppel Gate, Higher Ridgeway, Ottery St Mary, Devon EX11 1TJ   01404 814270 www.buildsomethingbeautiful.com

J and J Sharpe (builders, suppliers, contractors, cob and lime courses) Furzedon, Merton, Okehampton EX20 3DS   01805 603587

Somerset Master Thatchers Association: Ted Parks, Mead House, 104 Periton Lane, Minehead, TA24 8DZ   www.somersetmasterthtachers.co.uk

David and Glyn Tyler (builders in traditional materials): Church Cottage, Puddington, Tiverton EX16 8LW   01884 861095

Mike Wye Associates (natural building and decorating products, lime courses): Buckland Filleigh Sawmills, Devon EX21 5RN www.mikewye.co.uk 01409 281644

Bibliography

Beacham, Peter (Editor): *Devon Building, an Introduction to Local Traditions,* Devon Books, Tiverton, 1990 and 2005

Carew, Richard: *Survey of Cornwall 1602,* Tamar Books, Launceston, 2004

Cox, Jo and Thorp, John RL: *Devon Thatch,* Devon Books, Tiverton, 2001

Egeland, Pamela: *Cob and Thatch,* Devon Books, Tiverton, 1988

Hoskins, W G: *Devon,* David and Charles, Newton Abbot, 1954 and 2003

McCann, John: *Clay and Cob Buildings,* Shire Publications, Princes Risborough, 1983

Pevsner, Nikolaus: *The Buildings of England* series, county by county volumes, Penguin, London

Schofield, Jane: *Lime in Building: A Practical Guide,* Black Dog Press, Crediton, 1994, 2005

Schofield, Jane and Smallcombe, Jill: *Cob Buildings a Practical Guide,* Black Dog Press, Crediton, 2004

Weismann, Adam and Bryce, Katy: *Building with Cob: A Step by Step Guide,* Green Books, Dartington, 2006